# Beautiful Volcanoes
## For Kids!

## Nature Books for Kids
### By K. Bennett
### Mendon Cottage Books

*JD-Biz Publishing*

**Download Free Books!**
**http://MendonCottageBooks.com**

Read More Amazing Animal Books

Purchase at Amazon.com

# Table of Contents

# Introduction

*I see Earth! It is so beautiful!* ~ ***Yuri Gagarin***

***Volcanoes:*** Volcanoes are powerful openings on the surface of planet earth. They are like very big vents with lots of hot things boiling inside and sometimes these hot things spill over! Volcanoes can be fascinating and exciting but they can also be scary and very dangerous!

You might think of a Volcano like a big mountain but they are very different than the normal mountains we know about. What makes it different is what's inside. Have you ever looked inside a volcano? Neither have I!

### How are volcanoes different?

*Mountains:* A mountain is like a huge heap that comes out of the ground and is higher than the places around it. Do you know what mountains are made of? Yes! It's made of earth and rocks.

*Volcanoes:* These formations are very different. You might think of them as huge heaps that come out of the ground made of ash, magma, lava and dust! This makes Volcanoes very hot.

Lots of interesting things happens under, around and inside a Volcano and we will learn about most of them. Are you ready?

Volcanoes have a lot of energy and when they blow their top, ash, liquid rock, and poisonous gases explode into the air.

This is very dangerous for people and animals around the volcano, so they need to stay far away!

### Why does a Volcano blow its top?

*Easyscienceforkids.com* explains what happens in an easy way to understand…

*"Imagine a pot of chili bubbling on the stove. If it has a lid on it, steam can't escape. The chili might just bubble up and erupt over the sides of the pan. Take the lid off, though, and the heat can escape."*

### What happens when a Volcano blows its top?

If you dug all the way inside the earth, you would see something that looks like a giant puzzle with lots of different parts. The parts we want to know about are called: "tectonic plates."
There are eight important plates on the planet and there are some small ones too. These big plates move around all the time and soon pressure starts to build.

***Geography4kids.com*** says to think of the plates like the skin of planet earth.

When these plates move around, magma and gas inside the earth starts to get a little more intense. It gets hotter and hotter and the pressure gets bigger and bigger! Can you guess what happens next? Yes! A Volcano explodes.

When a volcano erupts, other things can happen at the same time too. Sometimes it can be earthquakes, tsunamis, floods, falling rocks or mud flows. If you lived near an exploding Volcano you would have to leave right away!

In this book, we will use some special words when we talk about volcanoes. You may not know what they mean so we will define them for you. For example, what is magma? What about lava?

Let's define the words so you can become an expert Volcanologist!

-**Vent:** A vent is an opening somewhere. In the case of Volcanoes this is an opening in the ground and it helps pressure, steam, air and ash to escape!

-**Magma**: The rocks inside the earth can get very hot. After they get too hot they turn into liquid. This liquid rock is called magma.

-*Erupt:* This just means something that blows up or explodes! It can also mean something that bursts into flames!

-*Lava:* When magma gets to the surface of the earth and into the atmosphere it is called lava!

-*Spew:* This means to throw something.

-*Toxic:* Something that's toxic is not good for people. It is very poisonous, can make us sick or even kill us!

-*Ash:* Rocks burn and the burnt parts turn into dust. This is called ash.

-*Escape:* This means to get away from somewhere dangerous fast!

-*Crater*: This looks like a big bowl on top of the volcano.

There are many other words that apply to volcano formations. How many more words can you add to this list?

Have fun researching and don't forget to get permission before you search!

### Why are Volcanoes special?

The soil around Volcanoes is great for planting and growing things! Volcanoes also lower the pressure inside the earth and help the tectonic plates to settle down. **Remember:** These plates are always moving around.

Let's learn more about volcanoes and how they make our planet so different from other places!

## DID YOU KNOW?

There are three different stages in a Volcano's life. They can be:

-Active

-Dormant or

-Extinct.

## *What's the difference?*

-An active volcano is very busy! It may have just erupted or blown its top. Or it may be in the process of erupting and blowing its top. What a busy volcano!

-A dormant volcano is asleep but can still erupt if it wakes up. Shhhhh… be very quiet!

-An extinct volcano is very different from the others. This type of volcano is what scientist think will never erupt again!

Source: www.ducksters.com

# Chapter 1: *Let's learn more!*

All right Volcanologist, let's dig deep into the earth's crust and see what else we can find!

*Different kinds of volcanoes*:

Just like most things on planet earth, volcanoes come in different kinds and sizes. Three of them are called: **Cinder Cone, Shield and Strato or Composite** volcanoes. What interesting names, don't you think? But each one is special in its own way.

Let's see how!

**Cinder Cone:** These volcanoes are not very big and the crater on top is small. These types of volcanoes don't have a lot of lava and the eruptions come just from one vent instead of many different ones!

**Strato or Composite volcanoes:** These volcanoes look like a cone but they take a long time to form. How long? Thousands and thousands of years! That's a very old volcano! They are made with layers and layers of lava and sand. They can also get very big over time, sometimes thousands of feet high. You might recognize the names of Mount Vesuvius, Mount St. Helens and Krakatoa.

*Shield:* This type of volcano can also get very big! They are mostly made of frozen lavas after it cools off. On the island of Hawaii, there is a very large shield volcano over 30,000 feet above sea level! These volcanoes have very large craters on the top and when it blows it can be a huge explosion!

## FUN FACTS!

Can you guess where the name Volcano comes from? It comes from the Romans. They worshipped a god by the name of Vulcan. Can you guess why this god was used to name a volcano? Think about it and find at the answer at the end of the book!

*How many volcanoes are on the planet?*

1-60,000


2-5,000


3-1,500


Which number did you choose? Was it number 3? Great job! If you want to be sure about this number go to the website: www.usgs.gov to learn more!

It is important to know that this number does not include the volcanoes on the ocean floor!

# Ring of Fire

Volcanoes are most active in a place called the Ring of Fire. Have you ever heard about this place before?

This ring is in the Pacific Ocean but you cannot see it with your eyes. Why not? Because it is under the ocean!

75% of volcano activity happens around these rings, so this part of the planet is always buzzing like a beehive!

80-90% of big earthquakes happen around this ring too!

How big is the ring in miles? Can you guess the number…

1-2,000 miles

2-25,000 miles

3-150,000 miles

The correct answer is….2! The ring is **25,000 miles** long! That's a very big ring!

Of course, the shape is not really a circle but looks more like a horseshoe.

There are approximately **452** volcanoes along the ring. To find them you would have to travel along South America, then up to the coast of North America, then across the Bering Strait and Japan and over to New Zealand. That's a lot of territory!

It is easier to follow the ring on a map. Ask your parent or a guardians permission to search for "Ring of fire" online. Then you can follow the trail of the most active volcanoes on planet earth!

(*Source:* http://education.nationalgeographic.com/encyclopedia/ring-fire/ )

Around the ring of fire you will find locations known as HOT SPOTS. These spots are very important. This is where the heat rises from inside the earth and melts the rocks on top. Do you remember what the melted rocks are called? Yes! Magma. Very good.

When these hot rocks start to push their way up to the surface, it forms a volcano. The great part about hot spots is that it doesn't really move the tectonic plates like other volcanoes, so scientists do not think of hot spots as part of the Ring of Fire.

Did you enjoy this first chapter on volcanoes? Learn anything new? I hope so! Now…let's talk about some very special volcanoes and how they "heat" up the world around us.

# Chapter 2 Volcanoes are powerful!

## 1 – *Mount Tambora*

One of the biggest volcanoes that ever blew its top was Mount Tambora in the year 1815 on April 10th.

It not only damaged the area where the volcano erupted but all around the world! It was so bad that many people call this eruption the "Pompeii of Indonesia." Some say the mountain blew its top off!

But how powerful was the explosion? People who lived in Sumatra more than 1,200 miles away heard it!!!

That is not all that happened. In 1816, the year after the eruption people had problems to find food to eat. Can you guess why? Because the eruption of Mount Tambora put so much ash into the air it blocked the sunlight from getting to the earth! The plants did not grow well and lots of people went hungry.

That year was called the "year without summer."

What a powerful explosion!

## 2 – *Mount Krakatoa*

Another big eruption happened in Indonesia on Mount Karakatoa in 1883. This eruption was so big it made 140 foot tsunami waves! Sadly, lots of people got hurt and the island where the mountain sat was totally destroyed by the explosion!

## 3 – *Mount Novarupta*

This eruption happened in the Alaskan peninsula. This volcano was part of a chain and in 1912 it blew miles of magma sky high! There was so much ash in the air that it covered 3,000 square miles and was one foot deep!

## 4 – *Mount Pinatubo*

This eruption created a huge pillar of ash 22 miles high! So much ash fell that many roofs collapsed under the weight. Millions of tons of sulfur dioxide went into the air and spread all over the world. This caused the temperature to drop about 1 degree the following year!

## 5 – *Mount Vesuvius*

This eruption is very famous and happened on August 24th of the year A.D. 79. When Mount Vesuvius blew its top it buried the city of Pompeii in 20 feet of ash.

The eruption started around noon but by 1:00 pm, you couldn't see the sun anymore because the ash was too strong.

The sea moved too! A man that wrote about history by the name of Pliny the Younger said, "the sea retreated as if pushed by earthquakes."
This makes us think of tsunamis when the sea moves away from the shore.

The wind was also very strong and lots of black clouds and smoke filled the air. This eruption was so powerful that we still remember it today!

(Source: www.livescience.com )

## DID YOU KNOW?

Volcanoes are measured on a scale just like earthquakes and hurricanes. But this scale has a different name. It is called: **Volcanic Explosivity Index** or VEI if that is easier to remember!

The scale runs from the numbers 1 to 8. Check out the list!

Number 1 – Gentle eruption. It can blow 100 – 1000 meters into the air. Stromboli is an example of this type of eruption.

Number 2 – Explosive.  It can blow 1-5 kilometers into the air. Galeras is an example of this type of eruption.

Number 3 – Severe. This can blow 3 – 15 kilometers into the air. Nevada del Ruiz is an example of this type of eruption.

Number 4 – Cataclysmic. This can blow 10 – 25 kilometers into the air. Galunggung is an example of this type of eruption.

Number 5 – Paroxysmal. This can blow more than 25 kilometers into the air. Mount St. Helens is an example of this type of eruption.

Number 6 – Colossal. This can blow more than 25 kilometers into the air. Krakatau is an example of this type of eruption.

Number 7 – Super Colossal. This can blow sky high or more than 25 kilometers into the air. Mount Tambora is an example of this type of eruption.

Number 8 – Mega Colossal. If you ever see this type of eruption you will know. The clouds will reach as far as the eye can see and way over 25 kilometers into the air! Yellowstone is an example of this type of eruption.

Source: (http://volcano.oregonstate.edu/how-big-are-eruptions )

# Chapter 3 More Explosive facts!

Now let's talk about some more explosive facts you may or may not know about!

- When volcanoes erupt and as the years go by, lots of interesting formations appear on the mountains and rocks.

*Volcanic rock:* There are many different types of volcanic rocks depending on the type of eruption. They have very complicated names but these might be easier for you: Pumice, Obsidian, Rhyolite and Basalt.

Let's learn more!

*Pumice:* This type of rock is formed by lava with lots of bubbles in it. When it cools, the rock is so light it can even float in water!

*Obsidian:* This type of rock is volcanic glass. It is usually black but there are some rocks in other colors like brown and green. There are even rare colors like blue, red, yellow and even orange!

*Ryholite:* This type of rock is really amazing. Did you know you can find gems in this volcanic rock? It has quartz in it and can be reddish, brown, green and tan colored. Gem rocks that come from this formation are called Wonderstone and Hickoryte. You can also make really decorations with this type or rocks!

**Basalt:** This is a hard rock and is used around the world to make statues and cobblestones! It is also very hard to break apart or crush. What interesting formations come from Volcanoes!

(Source: www.ehow.com )

Other neat formations!

Do you remember how a lava tube is formed? In our books *"Beautiful Caves for kids"* we talked about it! Here is a small part of what we wrote about:

*"Let's say a Volcano erupts and a tube of Lava flows down a hill. When it cools down and gets really hard, the inside of the Lava tube is hollow and this is where a Cave forms!"*

These tubes look very interesting but I don't know if I want to explore one...what about you?

-You might think of volcanoes as being very hot places, but volcanoes can be found in many different climates, even very cold ones. And many volcanoes have snow on the sides of the mountains.

How is that possible?
Do you remember where the heat comes from inside a volcano? Yes, from INSIDE the earth. So it is pretty nice on the outside until things get "heated" up!

-Do you remember how fertile the ground can be around volcanoes? Many people love to plant in this type of soil because things really grow well.

### Why is volcanic soil great for planting?

*Answer:* Because it is rich in calcium and lots of great minerals and microbes too!

Italy is a place where lots of things grow in rich volcanic soil. Things like: grapes, beans, cauliflower, onions, lemon trees and lots of tomatoes!

Did you know the most fragrant and best smelling flowers come from volcanic soil? Yes, they do!

- There are lots of big volcanoes on planet earth but did you know there is a huge volcano in space? It's on Mars and is around 374 miles wide and 13 miles high. It's called Olympus Mons! That's a very big volcano.

- Lots of volcanic gases mix together to form very dangerous fumes. Do you know what they are?

Here is a short list:

-Hydrogen sulfide

-Hydrogen chloride

-Sulfur dioxide

-Carbon dioxide and

-Hydrogen fluoride!

-Do you remember the volcanic rock Pumice? We just talked about it a moment ago. This type of rock is used in many beauty salons around the world to remove old or dry skin. Try it on your feet or heels. They will feel nice and soft when you are done!

And now for the answer to the question we talked about in the first chapter…Vulcan is the roman god of…. FIRE!!!

And that's why his named was used for Volcanoes.

## FUN FACTS!

Learn about the different levels of a volcano from the bottom all the way to the top.

Start with the **MAGMA CHAMBER**. This is the hot, boiling rock at the base of the volcano making its way up to the surface.

Then you will see some red lines that look like roots or branches. These are called **VENTS**.

Then the smoke coming out of the top is called: **ERUPTION CLOUD**.

And the top of the mountain is called: **CRATER.**

And the magma that flows up to the top and spills over the sides of the mountain is called: **LAVA FLOW.**

The ash and rock that mix together in the eruption cloud is called: **TEPHRA.**

And the layers of rocks and soil from inside the ground are called: **STRATA.**

Good job Volcanologists! Now you know a lot more about Volcanoes.

# Conclusion:

***In conclusion***:  Learning about volcanoes can be a fascinating adventure! Would you like to continue learning a little more about them?

***A creative idea for you!***

Pick a volcano, any volcano and ask yourself what makes it different from other volcanoes. Is it a shield, composite or cinder cone? What about a lava dome?

Research and find out what makes a lava dome special!

*More Ideas*:

Find out about volcanology terms like pyroclastic clouds or pyroclastic flows. Or find out how magma chambers work. Does it matter how runny and sticky it is? Can it stop an eruption or make it worse?

If you don't know where to look, ask your teacher, parent or guardian for help!

You can also use a volcano for show and tell. Do you know how to make one? Would you like to learn?

*Fun activity*:

This activity is listed at *Learningforkids.com* and it is a fun activity you can enjoy building with friends and family.

First you need to a place to build your volcano. After you choose a suitable place, these are the materials you will need:

-Plastic bottle – empty – 1 liter

-Newspaper torn into strips

-Craft glue – PVA is recommended but you may also have an idea!

-Masking tape

-Container to mix water and glue

For the lava you will need:

-Bicarbonate soda

-Red and yellow food coloring

-White vinegar

Are you ready to build? Great!

## Steps:

You have to cut out the middle part of the plastic bottle. Then overlap both ends, and join together with lots of masking tape. Use the newspaper to give your bottle a tube shape around the base just like a volcano. Keep wrapping until you get the shape you like!

Then use the newspaper to cover the WHOLE bottle and make a nice shaped volcano.

To add the newspaper strips you will need to get a little messy with the water and glue. Enjoy the challenge and build away!

When your volcano is completely dry, start to paint it with the colors you like. The recommendation is black, grey and a little brown but be creative. You might decide to do a purple volcano! The choice is yours.

*Lava:*

Try the sample listed at the website: Use 4 tablespoons of bicarbonate soda and 1 cup of vinegar. Don't forget to add the red and yellow die which will come out like an orange color.

Pour it inside the volcano with a funnel. Take out the funnel quickly and step back!!

Then watch your volcano erupt. On a scale of 1 to 8 how would you rate it?

Good job explorer!

(Source: http://www.learning4kids.net/2012/04/11/how-to-make-a-homemade-volcano/ )

*One final suggestion:*

Try becoming a junior storyteller and write about an extinct volcano and how it came back to life!

Here's how: Go online and see if you can find any stories about extinct volcanoes.  Build a story and imagine what would happen if it blew its top!

Don't forget to share share your ideas with others.

*Remember:* Sharing is caring!

I hope you enjoyed this book on **Beautiful Volcanoes** and always remember…

**"Educating the mind without educating the heart is no education at all."** *- Aristotle*

# Author Bio

K. Bennett loves to write for both children and adults. Many different subjects are interesting to develop, but writing for children is special to her heart.

Her favorite pastimes include reading, traveling and discovering new things. Each of these activities helps to fuel her imagination and acts like a blank canvas waiting for more stories.

She is intrigued with fantasy elements like hidden worlds and faraway lands. And basically anything that gets her imagination soaring to new heights!

Her writing credits include children books online and other writing works listed at Amazon.com

## Download Free Books!
## http://MendonCottageBooks.com

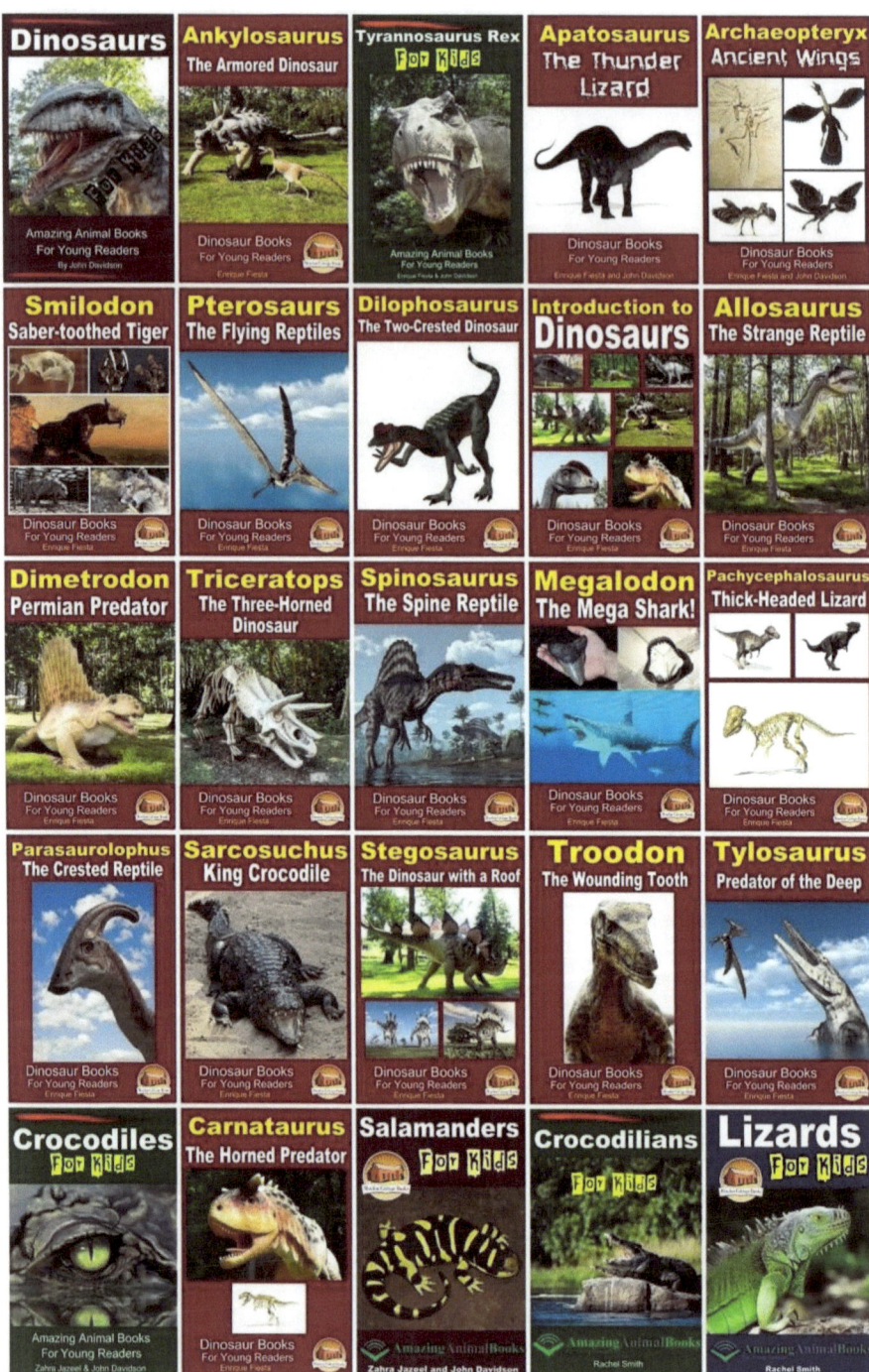

**Top Ten Dog Breeds For Kids**
Amazing Animal Books For Young Readers
Kisha Bennett & John Davidson

**German Shepherds**
Dog Books for Kids
K. Bennett

**Bulldogs**
Dog Books for Kids
K. Bennett

**Dachshund**
Dog Books for Kids
K. Bennett

**Poodles**
Dog Books for Kids
K. Bennett

**Labrador Retrievers**
Dog Books for Kids
K. Bennett

**Rottweilers**
Dog Books for Kids
K. Bennett

**Boxers**
Dog Books for Kids
K. Bennett

**Golden Retrievers**
Dog Books for Kids
K. Bennett

**Puppies**
Dog Books For Kids
Amazing Animal Books
By John Davidson

**Beagles**
Dog Books for Kids
K. Bennett

**Yorkshire Terriers**
Dog Books for Kids
K. Bennett

**Dogs**
Top Ten Dog Breeds For Kids
Amazing Animal Books For Young Readers
Zahra Jazeel & John Davidson

**Cats For Kids**
Amazing Animal Books For Young Readers
K. Bennett & John Davidson

**Foxes For Kids**
Amazing Animal Books For Young Readers
Zahra Jazeel & John Davidson

**Wolves For Kids**
Amazing Animal Books For Young Readers
By John Davidson and Virginia Fidler

# Publisher

JD-Biz Corp

P O Box 374

Mendon, Utah 84325

http://www.jd-biz.com/

**Download Free Books!**
**http://MendonCottageBooks.com**

---